HOW I GET AROUND

TRAINS

RYAN EARLEY

TABLE OF CONTENTS

A Pelican Book

SEAHORSE PUBLISHING

Teaching Tips for Caregivers and Teachers:

Research shows that one of the best ways for students to learn a new topic is to read about it.

Before Reading

- Read the title and predict what the book will be about.
- Read the "Words to Know" and discuss the meaning of each word.
- Read the back cover to see what the book is about.

During Reading

- When a student gets to a word that is unknown, ask them to look at the rest of the sentence to find clues to help with the meaning of the unknown word.
- Motivate students with praise and encouragement.

After Reading

- Discuss the main idea of the book.
- Ask students to give one detail that they learned in the book.

Sight Words

all
around
by
get
go
have
I
many
on
some

Words to Know

cars

chimneys

engines

tracks

train

wheels

I get around by **train**.

train

Many trains have **engines**.

engine
2402
KEEP CLEAR
DANGER AREA

chimney

Some trains have **chimneys**.

Some trains have many **cars**.

All train cars have **wheels**.

wheel

tracks

All trains go on **tracks**.

Index

Written by: Ryan Earley
Design by: Niko Magaro
Editor: Kim Thompson
Series Development: James Earley

Photos: All images from Shutterstock

Library of Congress PCN Data
Trains / Ryan Earley
How I Get Around
ISBN 979-8-8945-9256-5(hard cover)
ISBN 979-8-8945-9270-1(paperback)
ISBN 979-8-8945-9298-5(EPUB)
ISBN 979-8-8945-9284-8(eBook)
ISBN 979-8-8945-9312-8(audio)
ISBN 979-8-8945-9326-5(Read-Along)
Library of Congress Control Number: 2024946359

Printed in Canada/012025/CP20250101

Seahorse Publishing Company
seahorsepub.com

Published in the United States
Seahorse Publishing
PO Box 771325
Coral Springs, FL 33077

SEAHORSE PUBLISHING